Warships
fotofax

US NAVY
1942–1943
Robert C. Stern

GW00385439

Front cover illustration:
The battleship *Massachusetts* at
Casablanca; see illustration 50.

Back cover illustrations:
Top: The tower bridge of
Alabama (BB60) at Casco Bay,
Maine, January 1943. The
magenta cast of the signal flags,
which should be pure red,
indicates that the Sea Blue in this
Ms.12 Mod appears to be more
purplish than it was in reality.
Note the Mk 8 (FH) radar atop
the main battery director. (USN/
NARS)

Bottom: Having had her stocks
of ammunition depleted by
continual support activities off
Sicily, the light cruiser *Savannah*
(CL42) retired to Algiers for a
quick restock. There an oiler
caught fire on 13 July 1943,
providing a spectacular backdrop
for this view of the cruiser in Ms.
22. The proper yellow-orange
hue of the fire indicates that the
colour balance of this photo is
correct. (USN/NARS)

1. The heavy cruiser *Indianapolis* (CA35) off Attu, 8 June 1943; the *Omaha* Class light cruisers *Raleigh* (CL7), *Detroit* (CL8) and *Richmond* (CL9) steam an opposite course in the background. These four old cruisers formed the core of a fire support group that saw action during the reconquest of the Aleutians. The Japanese captured the islands of Attu and Kiska in early June 1942 as part of a failed attempt to distract the attention of the Americans from the Midway attack. The campaign to recapture the two insignificant tundra islands took over a year and occupied significant numbers of the older ships of the US Navy. (USN/NARS)

ARMS AND
ARMOUR

US NAVY
1942–1943

Robert C. Stern

2. A moment of highest drama: a 'Val' dives on the carrier *Enterprise* (CV6) as she twists between the splashes of near-misses during the Battle of Santa Cruz, 26 October 1942. Smoke rises from two bomb hits forward that caused minor damage but failed to knock *Enterprise* out of the fight. (USN/NARS)

3. After the dramatic engagement at Midway, the US Navy paused only briefly to reorganize, and immediately began deploying its forces to the South Pacific in anticipation of the attempt to recapture the Solomons. The principal units of the reorganized Pacific Fleet were the four task forces centred on the remaining fleet aircraft carriers. TF11 was based on *Saratoga* (CV3), which returned from repairs just days too late to participate in the Battle of Midway. She is seen pulling into Pearl Harbor on 6 June 1942, two days after the famous battle. (USN/NARS)

▲2   ▼3

INTRODUCTION

First published in Great Britain in 1990 by Arms and Armour Press, Artillery House, Artillery Row, London SW1P 1RT.

Distributed in the USA by Sterling Publishing Co. Inc., 387 Park Avenue South, New York, NY 10016–8810.

Distributed in Australia by Capricorn Link (Australia) Pty. Ltd, P.O. Box 665, Lane Cove, New South Wales 2066, Australia.

British Library Cataloguing in Publication Data
Stern, Robert C. (Robert Cecil) 1946–
US Navy 1942–1943.
1. United States. Navy. Warships, history
I. Title II. Series
623.8'25'0973
ISBN 0-85368-944-X

Designed and edited by DAG Publications Ltd. Designed by David Gibbons; edited by Roger Chesneau; layout by Cilla Eurich; typeset by Ronset Typesetters Ltd, Darwen, Lancashire, and Typesetters (Birmingham) Ltd, Warley, West Midlands.

At Midway the seemingly irresistible tide of Japanese advance was brought to an emphatic halt. By a combination of excellent intelligence and just plain luck, the harried forces marshalled by the US Navy north of Hawaii in early June 1942 tore the heart out the Japanese carrier striking force and left both sides wondering what could come next. From the American side, the Japanese may have looked as if they were marching to some master plan, but in fact the swift advances following the attack on Pearl Harbor took them as much by surprise as they did the Americans. The direction of those advances was more a result of momentum than conscious thought. The over-ambitious plan that took Japanese naval forces to the Aleutians and the Hawaiian Islands in June 1942 also took them to the southern Solomon Islands, where they set up a seaplane base in the protected waters off tiny Tulagi island and began the construction of an airfield on the island of Guadalcanal across Savo Sound.

The Allies had to react to this move. With Hawaii free from threat after Midway, the next concern was the safety of the supply line to Australia. The move into the Solomons directly threatened the sea lane that led from Hawaii to the east coast of Australia by way of Samoa, Fiji and New Caledonia. Victory at Midway left the momentum in the hands of the Allies. Plans rapidly evolved to set US Marines ashore on Guadalcanal and put the almost completed airfield there to use against its former owners. Yet in the uncertain balance of forces that existed after Midway, each move seemed to draw its inevitable countermove. Neither side could afford to let the other gain an easy victory in the Solomons. The result was a 'meatgrinder' campaign that continued to build with a logic of its own until one side or the other would flinch, finally concluding that the price that would have to be paid to keep control of this patch of malarial jungle and jagged mountain was too high. The naval battle of attrition that transpired was to the taste of neither side, but it inevitably favoured the Allies. A campaign that traded ship for ship had to be won by the side with more hulls. Along the way, there were fought two major carrier battles and countless desperate night battles in the narrow waters of Savo Sound. So vicious and so costly were these night engagements for control of the waters off Guadalcanal that Savo Sound was renamed, in the minds of American sailors, Ironbottom Bay.

This second volume on the US Navy in the Second World War primarily covers this Solomons Campaign that began with the preparations for Operation 'Watchtower', the invasion of Guadalcanal, in August 1942 and effectively ended with the invasion of Cape Gloucester at the tip of New Britain on the day after Christmas in 1943. Against this main theme of action in the South Pacific will be balanced the other campaigns that were also played out during late 1942 and 1943. While the bloody sea battles in the Solomons were being fought, US naval forces also saw action in the frigid Aleutians and the no less inhospitable Atlantic. By the time this critical period drew to a close, the Allies had turned the tide on all fronts. Major battles remained to be fought, brave sailors would die and brave ships would sink in flames, but the result was no longer in doubt and the identity of the inevitable victor was known to all.

Robert C Stern

▲4

▲5   ▼6

4. The small fleet carrier *Wasp* (CV7), seen here off Hampton Roads on 26 May 1942, was hastily transferred from the Atlantic to help make up for the loss of *Lexington at Coral Sea and Yorktown* at Midway. On 10 June she passed along the Panama Canal and became the centre of the newly formed TF18. Note the CXAM-1 antenna on her foremast; *Wasp* was one of only fourteen ships to receive this early air search radar. (USN/NARS)

5. Another recent transfer from the Atlantic Fleet with *Wasp* was the new battleship *North Carolina* (BB35), seen here on 10 June 1942. She stayed only briefly as part of *Wasp*'s escort, soon transferring to TF16 with *Enterprise*. Like most Atlantic Fleet ships of the time, she wore an early version of Ms. 12 Mod. She also has a CXAM-1 antenna. (USN/NARS)

6. The amphibious forces earmarked for the landings on Guadalcanal and Tulagi in Operation 'Watchtower' finished their training in the islands of Tonga and then advanced to meet their escort forces in the Fiji area in late July. This view shows some of the assembled forces at Fiji, seen from *Enterprise*. A *Mahan* Class destroyer is seen over the mid-section of another of the same class. Further in the background is an *Astoria* class heavy cruiser; six of the seven units of that class were here. (USN/NARS)

7. Also assembling were the reconstituted remnants of the Allied Asian Fleet, which had been driven back to Australia in the opening days of the war. Now composed of cruisers and destroyers (mostly RAN ships), this unit formed TG62.2 of the invasion fleet, responsible for the close escort of the landing force. HMAS *Canberra* is seen here from *Enterprise* in the Fiji area, 22 July 1942. (USN/NARS)

8. The invasion force for 'Watchtower' left Fiji at the end of July. These four APDs, old destroyers converted to fast attack transports, photographed from *Chicago* (CA29) on 26 July 1942, formed the lead element of the Tulagi landing force. The APDs are making a line-ahead turn to bring them on to a course parallel to *Chicago*. A *Craven* Class destroyer escorts in the background. (USN/NARS)

9. Another old US heavy cruiser, *Salt Lake City* (CA25) watches the invasion force leave Fiji. The transit from Fiji to the Solomons proved uneventful: the Japanese had no inkling that an invasion was afoot and consequently made no attempt to hinder its approach. The strength of their reaction after the landing would lead one to believe that, had they known of the invasion force, they would have made the approach to the Solomons a bloody affair. (USN/NARS)

7▲

8▲   9▼

▲10

▲11 ▼12

10. TG61.1 was the old TF16 formed around *Enterprise* (CV6), one of three carriers providing escort to the 'Watchtower' fleet. *Enterprise* herself is on the horizon to the left of this photograph. The new anti-aircraft cruiser *Atlanta* (CL51) is in the foreground; she had already seen action at the Battle of Midway and would be active in the South Pacific during her short career. (USN/NARS)

11. The fleet of APs stands off Lunga Point, Guadalcanal, after depositing its load of Marines, 7 August 1942. Nearly all the 'defenders' encountered on Guadalcanal were impressed Korean labourers who took to the hills as soon as the Marines landed. (USN/NARS)

12. The Japanese reaction was swift. On the same day, a force of 27 'Bettys', nine 'Vals' and eighteen Zeros flew from Rabaul to attack the transports. For the 'Vals', the trip was one-way because they had insufficient range to return. This view shows 'Betty' twin-engine bombers, just visible as tiny silhouettes against the horizon, heading into Lunga Roads amidst flak bursts. A *Craven* Class destroyer defends in the foreground, as seen from *Chicago* (CA29). (USN/NARS)

13. A 'Betty' (G4M1) passes close over *Chicago* on her way in to attack the APs. Between the attack on the 7th and a repeat attack the next day, the Japanese managed to sink one AP and damage two destroyers, one of which was later sunk by Japanese aircraft. The losses in aircraft were too high for these attacks to continue on a regular basis. If the Japanese had wanted to hold Guadalcanal – and they definitely did – they would have had to contest for the waters around the island with naval surface and air forces. (USN/NARS)

14. The reason for the importance of Guadalcanal lay in a small dirt runway airfield nearing completion at Lunga Point. Quickly finished by American engineers, and equally quickly dubbed 'Henderson Field', it became home to a small force of Navy and Marine pilots and their Dauntlesses and Wildcats. Equally important was its utility as a refuelling and rest stop for carrier scout and attack planes; this SBD-3 is probably from VB-3 or VS-3 off *Saratoga*. The Japanese understood its importance: most of the night engagements off Guadalcanal started as Japanese attempts to shell the field into submission. (USMC)

15. The Japanese naval reaction was not long in coming. Almost as soon as word of landing arrived at Rabaul, a force of five heavy cruisers, two light cruisers and a single destroyer under Admiral Mikawa headed south to take on the invasion force. The Allied commanders expected such a reaction and disposed an almost equivalent force under Rear-Admiral Crutchley RN across the northern entrance to Savo Sound. By midnight on 8/9 August, the Japanese forces were only 35 miles north of Savo Island. Crutchley was concerned with covering the landing forces at Lunga Point and Tulagi, splitting his forces into three separate groups with two radar picket destroyers just to the north-west of Savo. The Japanese forces in line ahead had no radar but their superior night fighting equipment, training and skill

13▲

14▲   15▼

allowed them to slip past the picket destroyers without being observed. The first Allied force encountered by Mikawa was composed of the heavy cruisers *Chicago* (CA29) and *Canberra*

(seen here off Tulagi) and two destroyers. At 0143 *Canberra* was hit by a pair of torpedoes and smothered in 8in gunfire from the van cruisers of the Japanese line and disabled before she

could reply; *Chicago* was hit by a single torpedo just minutes later and was likewise knocked out of action. (USN/NARS)

▲16

▲17 ▼18

16. Mikawa swung to the north, next encountering a force of three USN heavy cruisers – *Astoria* (CA34, seen here from *Chicago* en route to Guadalcanal), *Quincy* (CA39) and *Vincennes* (CA44) – and two more destroyers. This ill-fated group was overwhelmed when Japanese torpedoes and gunfire struck without warning out of the night. All three cruisers were soon reduced to floating wreckage. (USN/NARS)

17. The third group of Allied forces was composed of the light cruisers *San Juan* (CL45, seen here in the Tulagi area) and *Hobart*. Being further to the south, this group missed the Japanese onslaught and escaped damage, unaware of the havoc being wreaked only miles away. (USN/NARS)

18. Mikawa withdrew to the north, satisfied that he had accomplished his mission. He left four Allied heavy cruisers sinking in his wake. *Quincy* and *Vincennes* sank before sunrise on the 9th. Dawn found *Canberra* burning, out of control – the destroyers *Blue* and *Patterson* (DD392) are seen here taking off her crew – and soon afterwards *Ellet* (DD398) sank her with torpedoes. *Astoria* briefly looked salvageable. Her fires were brought under control by mid-morning and she was taken under tow, but in the event she proved too badly damaged. Just after noon she capsized and sank. *Chicago* was towed to safety, but she was out of action for five months. Mikawa had taught the Americans a hard lesson in night fighting but had ultimately failed because he had not disrupted the landings on Guadalcanal. The Allies hurriedly finished unloading the transports off Lunga Point and did withdraw the next day, temporarily abandoning the Marines. (USN/NARS)

19. The first of those major carrier battles was in the Eastern Solomons, which occurred at the end of August as the result of a Japanese attempt to reinforce their troops on Guadalcanal. The

Japanese covered the move with their two remaining fleet carriers (*Shokaku* and *Zuikaku*) and used a light carrier, *Ryujo*, as a diversion. The Americans reacted with three of the four fleet carriers left after Midway, *Saratoga* (CV3), *Enterprise*(CV6) and *Wasp* (CV7). After groping for each other throughout the 22nd and 23rd, the opposing sides made contact on the 24th. American aircraft found *Ryujo* with a light escort at 1600 and made short work of her. Meanwhile, a force of 39 Japanese aircraft caught *Enterprise*. She is seen here from *Portland* (CA33) as she manoeuvres at high speed while a 'Val' dive bomber presses home its attack directly above the aft flight deck. (USN/NARS)

19▲

20. Most of the attacking Japanese fell victim to the CAP or to *Enterprise*'s deadly AA fire. One such was this 'Val', seen from *Enterprise* on its way to an encounter with the South Pacific. Despite the effective defence, *Enterprise* was hit by three bombs aft, but none caused serious damage and she was out of action only briefly. This battle went into the books as an American victory. The Japanese lost *Ryujo* and over 30 valuable aircraft and caused only minor damage on *Enterprise* in return. (USN/NARS)

21. In the next three weeks, Japanese submarines did what their carriers had failed to do. On 31 August 1942, *I26* put a torpedo in *Saratoga* (CV3) and knocked her out of the war again. Just over two weeks later, on 15 September, *I19* more than evened the score with a single salvo of six torpedoes. The carriers *Wasp* (CV7) and *Hornet* (CV8) were the only fleet carriers left in the South Pacific and they were on patrol off the Solomons covering yet another reinforcement convoy. Firing a full spread of potent 'Long Lance' torpedoes at *Wasp*, *I19* got three hits, sufficient to doom the carrier; the latter is seen here burning fiercely soon after being hit. (USN/NARS)

20▲　　21▼

▲22

22. The three torpedoes that missed *Wasp* were still to be heard from. Covering the ten miles that separated the two carrier groups, one torpedo passed directly under two destroyers before hitting the battleship *North Carolina* (BB55) on her port bow below the armour belt. The damage was not major but was enough to keep her out of action for five months. Another torpedo slammed into the bow of the destroyer *O'Brien* (DD415); this photograph shows the ship the next day at Espiritu Santo with a chunk of her bow missing. She was hastily patched up and judged sound enough to return to the USA on her own. That judgement was faulty: off Samoa, she began to break up, and she finally sank on 19 October, the last victim of *I19*'s remarkable salvo. (USN/NARS)

23. *Laffey* (DD459), one of *Wasp*'s escorts, pulls into Espiritu Santo loaded to the gunwales with survivors, 16 September 1942. She wears a weatherbeaten Ms. 11 camouflage. Like many of the original batch of destroyers committed to the Solomons, she had a busy, but brief, career. She saw almost continual action until her loss at the First Naval Battle of Guadalcanal in November. (USN/NARS)

24. The next major engagement came a month later off Cape Esperance, the northern tip of Guadalcanal. Both sides simultaneously ran reinforcement convoys to the island on the night of 11/12 October 1942. The Japanese escorted their transports with two destroyers and three heavy cruisers; the Americans opposed with two heavy cruisers, two light cruisers and five destroyers. Radar helped the Americans, under Rear Admiral Scott, to cut across the head of the Japanese line, bringing their lead ships under concentrated fire. *Farenholt* (DD491) is seen here as she appeared at the time, painted in the rare Ms. 15 camouflage. She led two other van destroyers between the two lines, a most unlucky place to get caught. She was hit by four large shells, probably American, and was forced to retire. In this view, *Farenholt* carries a Mk 4 (FD) radar atop her DP director; most US destroyers were radar-equipped by this time. (USN/NHC)

23▲   24▼

▲25

25. Running back to the north, the fleeing Japanese were still able to inflict serious damage on the Americans. The light cruiser *Boise* (CL47) switched on a searchlight to illuminate a suspected target but was herself hit repeatedly and forced out of the fight. The Solomons veteran *Buchanan* (DD484), shown here, was at the rear of the American line throughout the battle, escaping this engagement without a scratch. (USN/NARS)

26. Sometimes major enemy forces sortied and there were simply no ships available to counter them. The Japanese sent their carriers out in mid-October, supporting yet another reinforcement attempt. The only US forces out were a pair of destroyers escorting a fleet tug and a pair of APs towing avgas barges en route to Guadalcanal. When the Japanese carriers were detected, one destroyer and the APs turned back, but the avgas was needed at Henderson Field so desperately that one barge was transferred to the tug and the run continued with *Meredith* (DD434), shown here, as the remaining escort. On 15 October 1942 aircraft from *Zuikaku* caught the pair off San Cristobal and made quick work of them. (USN/NHC)

▼ 26

27. The next time the Japanese carriers sortied, barely a week later, the Americans were ready to react. The result was the Battle of Santa Cruz. The Japanese again had their two fleet carriers *Shokaku* and *Zuikaku* in the field, this time joined by the large merchant conversion *Junyo* and the light carrier *Zuiho*; to oppose them, the US Navy had *Hornet* (CV8) and *Enterprise* (CV6), the latter just back from hasty repairs. After a day of groping for each other on the 25th, scouts from the two sides found each other almost simultaneously just before 0700 on 26 October 1942. The Japanese were the first to get a strike off. When those aircraft arrived just after 1000, *Enterprise* was hidden in the rain squall that can be seen to the right in this view looking aft from *San Juan* (CL54). Note the flak bursts visible on the horizon. With *Enterprise* hidden, the Japanese struck elsewhere. (USN/NARS)

28. The Japanese concentrated on *Hornet*, putting at least five bombs and two torpedoes into her before retiring at 1020; additionally, a damaged 'Kate' torpedo bomber crashed into the port forward 5in gallery and exploded in the forward lift shaft, causing most of the smoke visible here. *Hornet* was left without power, with serious fires forward and a 7-degree list to port, but, despite appearances, she was still in a basically sound condition. (USN/NARS)

▲29 ▼30

29. The destroyer *Russell* (DD414) edged alongside *Hornet* to add its hoses to the fire-fighting effort as soon as the Japanese aircraft had retired at approximately 1030. The combined efforts of *Russell*, *Morris* (DD417) and *Hornet*'s own crew soon had the fires under control. Still afloat and in no danger of sinking, the carrier was nevertheless out of action for the day. (USN/NARS)

30. At 1030 *Enterprise* began landing aircraft from her own and *Hornet*'s scout and CAP missions in order to make room for returning strike aircraft. The American strike had been almost a complete failure, most aircraft never even finding the Japanese fleet. One group only, *Enterprise*'s SBDs, found *Shokaku* and set her on fire; like *Hornet*, she was out of action for the day. The second wave of Japanese attackers arrived overhead at 1115, this time finding *Enterprise*. Owing, in part, to the presence of *San Juan* and *South Dakota* (BB57) in her screen (both visible in this view to the right), the AA fire thrown up by the defenders was largely effective. (USN/NARS)

31. A 'Kate' torpedo bomber banks toward *Enterprise*'s stern in a photograph taken from *Portland* (CA33). Having dropped its torpedo, the 'Kate' turned towards its target, an unusual move probably motivated by the presence of escorts blocking all other escape routes. The torpedo missed, as did all others aimed at *Enterprise* that day. (USN/NARS)

32, 33. By an extraordinary coincidence, a photographer on board *Enterprise* was able to get two photographs of the 'Kate' as it passed up her port side and, dodging flak bursts, overflew an escorting destroyer before making good its escape. Japanese carrier aircraft at this stage of the war were painted dark green, with light grey under the wings and horizontal tail. Large red *hinomarus* (literally 'rising suns', called 'meatballs' by the Americans) were painted near the wing tips. (USN/NARS)

31▲

32▲   33▼

▲ **34**

34. A pair of 'Vals' suffer different fates after attempting to deliver their bombs on *Enterprise*. One heads toward the water in flames, having been hit by the heavy AA fire from *South Dakota*, seen just to the left of *Enterprise* in this view; the second 'Val', just visible in the upper right of this photograph, pulls out of its dive still in one piece. Their bombs suffered similar fates: they both near-missed. (USN/NARS)

35. Only two bombs hit *Enterprise* during this second wave of attacks. One hit just aft of the forward elevator and, the other hit the flight deck among the recently landed scout planes, setting one of the parked aircraft on fire. During the violent turns of her evasive manoeuvres and the jolts resulting from numerous near-misses, this SBD was pitched overboard near the aft end of *Enterprise*'s flight deck. (USN/NARS)

▼ **35**

36. Even destroyers contributed to the formidable AA defence that saved *Enterprise*. This *Mahan* Class destroyer adds its part to the general effort as it steams at high speed close to the carrier. One of *Enterprise*'s escorting destroyers, *Smith* (DD378), was hit bodily by a 'Kate'; another, *Porter* (DD356), was hit by a torpedo from *I21* and sank. The cruiser *Portland* was also hit by three torpedoes from the same source, but by pure luck they were fired at too short a distance and failed to arm. (USN/NARS)

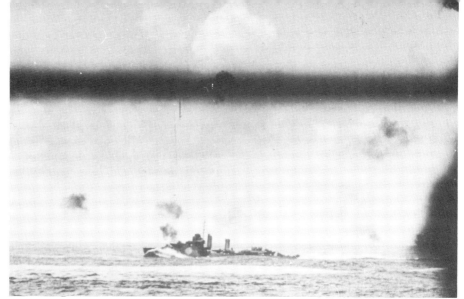

36▲

37. By 1100 all the fires on *Hornet* were under control and she was taken under tow by the heavy cruiser *Northampton* (CA26). The pair were only able to manage 4 knots and at that pace they would not be out of danger until well after nightfall. Note the bomb holes in the carrier's flight deck. (USN/NARS)

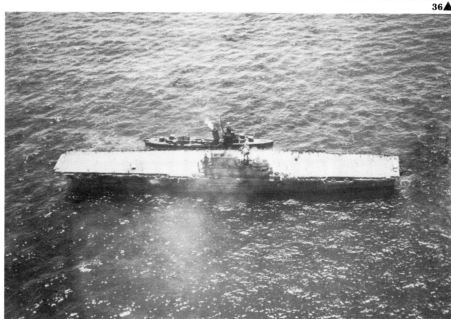

37▲　　**38▼**

38. By about 1600 *Hornet*'s engineers had managed to jury-rig an arrangement that bypassed the flooded compartments and got the carriers's engines going again; this in turn powered her generators and allowed her to start pumping out her flooded spaces. With such optimistic news, *Northampton* loosed her tow and *Hornet* prepared to get under way on her own power. (USN/NARS)

▲39

▲40　▼41

39. Luck was not with the Americans that day. Barely 20 minutes after *Hornet* began raising steam, another wave of Japanese aircraft, nine 'Kates' from *Junjo*, arrived overhead. They managed only one torpedo hit, but that was enough, flooding the remaining engine room and increasing the list to 18 degrees. (USN/NARS)

40. By 1655 the situation was obviously hopeless, and the order to abandon *Hornet* was given. The escorts that had previously helped her fight so valiantly now

took off her crew. She did not succumb easily. While the evacuation was under way six 'Bettys' from Rabaul put another torpedo into her, while at 1802 four 'Vals' from *Zuikaku* found her and put another bomb into her forward of the island. *Mustin* (DD413) and *Anderson* (DD411) were given the sad task of finishing her off with gunfire and torpedoes but were unable to complete the job before being driven off by the approaching Japanese, and the destroyers *Akigumo* and *Makigumo* completed the job with four

more torpedoes. The final score for the engagement favoured the Japanese: with *Hornet* sunk, the US Navy had only the damaged *Enterprise* in the South Pacific. But the Japanese could not take advantage of the situation. They had two of their four carriers at Santa Cruz badly damaged and had lost nearly their entire carrier air force to the deadly defence. It would take them longer to recover than the Americans. (USN/NARS)

41. Constant action, and the attrition that comes with it,

riveted the attention of the US Navy firmly on the South Pacific, yet action continued in other theatres. In the Atlantic, the primary occupation of the Navy was escorting merchant convoys and beginning the slow process of building up for the first invasion of Nazi-held territory. Most of the ships involved in this process were too old to be of use in the Pacific. One such was *Texas* (BB35) – seen here at Norfolk on 19 August 1942 – which was used extensively as convoy escort. (USN/NARS)

42. The small aircraft carrier *Ranger* (CV4) was kept in the Atlantic because she was considered too small and too slow to survive in the Pacific. In the Atlantic she was used primarily as an aircraft transport, carrying loads of Army Air Corps P-40s to be flown off to Accra en route to India. Here *Ranger* reloads an SB2U of her own air group on 26 August 1942. (USN/NARS)

▲ 43

43. The reconquest of Europe began with the invasion of Axis-held North Africa, Operation 'Torch'. This invasion was to be a joint affair. The Americans had responsibility for three Atlantic coast landings, the Royal Navy for the Mediterranean. The US Navy's invasion convoys

▼ 44

assembled on the east coast of the USA and made their way across the Atlantic under heavy escort. One such convoy is seen here under the watchful eye of *Texas* (BB35).

44. The new destroyer *Macomb* (DD458) was already an experienced anti-submarine escort when she was employed as screen for the northern task force heading for Mehdia in Morocco; another destroyer replenishes from an oiler in the background. Every precaution was taken to

ensure the safe passage of these convoys (for example, the routes chosen for them avoided the normal merchant convoy routes), and in the event the precautions proved effective: the convoys arrived off the African coast unobserved by the enemy. (USN/NARS)

458

45. The destroyer *Ellyson* (DD454) steams close by the escort carrier *Santee* (CVE29) en route to the 'Torch' landings, early November 1942. These ships were part of the centre group assigned to the attack on Fedala and Casablanca. *Santee* was one of the four large CVEs assigned to the convoy escort; these were fleet oiler conversions almost as large as the smaller purpose-built fleet carriers such as *Ranger* (CV4) and *Wasp* (CV7). (USN/NARS)

46. The southern task force was assigned to the attack on Safi on the morning of the 'Torch' invasion, 8 November 1942. This part of the attack was led by a pair of old 'four-piper' destroyers that had been specifically modified to carry the lead assault troops to the Moroccan port. Like most other modernized US Navy destroyers of First World War vintage, these two had their fourth, aftermost funnel removed and the armament of single 5in mounts reduced; they further had all loose tophamper and masts removed, to reduce their vulnerability to defensive fire. This view shows *Cole* (DD155), which carried troops from the 47th Infantry for an assault on the mole, assigned to the task of seizing the docks so that Allied armour could be easily offloaded. (USN/NARS)

47. A second old destroyer, *Bernadou* (DD153), was similarly modified for the assault on Safi. She carried two companies of troops of the 47th for the assault on the beach just south of the dock area. Both destroyers accomplished their missions. *Cole*'s troops seized the docks and their vital cranes, while *Bernadou*'s quickly gained control of the beach. *Cole* came through the affair without a scratch, while *Bernadou* was deliberately beached but suffered only minor damage. (USN/NARS)

45▲

46▲   47▼

▲48

48. The attack on Casablanca, the main city on the Atlantic coast of Morocco, concentrated on putting troops ashore on the beaches of Fedala, just north of the city. The cruiser *Augusta* (CA31) is seen here positioned among the attack transports that carried the 20,000 US Army troops tasked with the conquest of Casablanca. The Vichy French Navy reacted strongly to the appearance of the invasion fleet off Fedala: shortly after 0800, two destroyer leaders and five destroyers sortied from Casablanca and headed north along the coast. (USN/NARS)

▲49   ▼50

49. Part of the fire support group assigned to the Fedala landings, *Swanson* (DD443) had a busy day on 8 November. Coming under fire at first light while positioned close off-shore as beach guide, she duelled with coastal batteries until they were silenced and then took on the sortie of Vichy French destroyers toward Fedala later in the morning. The two destroyer leaders and five destroyers sailed from the port of Casablanca toward the landing beaches at 0825, still ignorant of the identity of the attackers. The two light cruisers and four destroyers of the fire support group (including *Swanson*) intercepted the six intruders. Ten minutes of long-range fire were sufficient to convince the French that their attack was futile, and they turned back towards the port. (USN/NARS)

50. The approaching Americans hoped that the traditional friendship with the French would be enough to prevent a fight between the invaders and the Vichy troops, and everything, including the new battleship *Massachusetts* (BB59), was festooned with multiple American flags. In the event, the French put up only token resistance in most cases, especially after the identity of the invaders became known. (USN/NHC)

51. The incomplete French battleship *Jean Bart*, tied up in the port at Casablanca, represented a major threat to the invasion. While a sortie in her unfinished state was never a real possibility, her one completed main battery turret held four 15in guns which could add considerable weight to the defence of the port. The Allies hoped *Jean Bart* would remain silent, but *Massachusetts* was on hand in case she did not. (NASM)

51▲

52. In the event, *Jean Bart* opened fired on the American covering forces at 0700 and *Massachusetts* responded with a murderous fire from her own nine 16in guns. When the Americans occupied Casablanca on 11 November 1942 they found the French battleship to be severely damaged, her deck buckled and her side plating blown out forward. Despite the extensive damage above the waterline, she was still basically sound, and she was eventually completed in 1949. (NASM)

52▼

US NAVY CAMOUFLAGE, 1942–3

The colours used in US Navy surface ship camouflage during the Second World War were all part of a series of paints mixed from varying amounts of white base stock and a dark blue-black tinting material. Depending on the amount of tinting material used, the colours that resulted ranged from pale grey to dark purple-blue in hue. Those used during this period were:

Haze Gray (5-H) A very pale neutral grey, made of a 1:20 proportion of tint to white.

Ocean Gray (5-O) Somewhat less pale, more noticeably cool-tinted, made of a 1:8 proportion of tint to white.

Sea Blue (5-S) Medium blue-grey, made of a 1:4 tint to white. This colour was officially replaced in June 1942 by Navy Blue.

Navy Blue (5-N) A somewhat darker purple-blue, made of a 1.5:4 tint to white.

The camouflage schemes used during the war by the US Navy for surface ships were less attempts to hide ships than efforts to make the exact identification and location of ships more difficult. After all, ships move, leave wakes, reflect the sun, cast shadows, etc., all of which make hiding a major combat ship essentially impossible. Further, as the war progressed, the increasing capabilities of shipborne radars made any attempt to hide a ship fruitless. However, an effective camouflage scheme could still make the job of an enemy submarine, surface ship or aircraft more difficult by making the exact size, range, course and speed harder to determine by visual means.

In general, camouflage schemes can be optimized to make the job of targeting more difficult for aircraft, for surface or for sub-surface threats, not for all three. Aircraft see ships against the dark background of water. Range, course and speed are essentially impossible to hide from an airborne antagonist, but a dark colour can make the ship blend into the sea and make its exact dimensions difficult to ascertain. The most effective anti-air camouflage schemes are those using solid dark colours. Sub-surface observers see ships against the background of horizon and sky, and so horizontally banded schemes that range from dark to light tend to be the most effective. The most difficult task is to attempt to produce a camouflage scheme effective against surface opponents. In this case, the option adopted by the US Navy was to attempt to confound enemy observers with 'dazzle' type schemes that would confuse rangefinding at close range and resolve to an overall purple-blue effect at longer ranges.

The camouflage measures used during this period were:

Ms.11 (Sea Blue System) Sea Blue (5-S) on all vertical surfaces. This and all measures had Deck Blue (20-B) on all horizontal surfaces. Primarily an anti-air system, this scheme was authorized in September 1941 and was theoretically superseded by Ms.21 in June 1942, but many ships, particularly auxiliaries, continued to wear it until at least the end of the year.

Ms.12 (Graded System) Sea Blue (5-S) up to the level of the main deck, following the sheer line of the deck, Ocean Gray (5-O) up to the level of the top of the superstructure, and Haze Gray

BUCHANAN (DD484), 1942

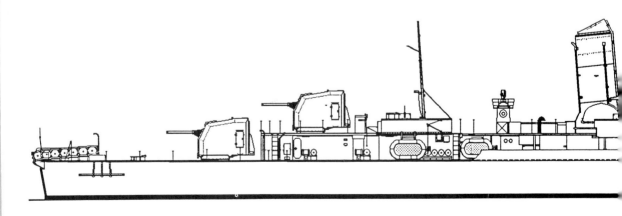

US NAVY SENSORS, 1942–3

(5-H) above. Primarily an anti-submarine system, this scheme was authorized in September 1941 and was theoretically superseded by Ms.22 in June 1942.

Ms.12 Mod ('Splotch') The same colours as standard Ms.12 but with wavy or 'sawtooth' edges between the colours. Later versions added 'splotches' of colour to achieve a more blended appearance in an attempt to make Ms.12 more effective against surface ships.

Ms.15 (Disruptive System) A graded system similar to Ms.12 Mod but substituting Navy Blue (5-N) for Sea Blue. Used more intentionally patterned designs as opposed to the often haphazard 'splotching' of Ms.12 Mod. Applied only to a few ships during 1942.

Ms.17 (Dazzle System) A similar scheme using hard angles and straight lines as opposed to the fluid shapes of Ms.15. Used only on a few ships during 1942.

Ms.21 (Navy Blue System) Navy Blue (5-N) on all vertical surfaces. Primarily an anti-air scheme. Authorized in June 1942 and used mainly in the Pacific.

Ms.22 (Graded System) Navy Blue (5-N) up to the lowest point of main deck, following the line of the horizon, with the remaining vertical surfaces Haze Gray (5-H). Primarily an anti-submarine scheme, this measure was authorized in June 1942 and used mainly in the Atlantic.

Designation	Type	Antenna	Comments
CXAM-1	AS	17ft × 18ft mattress	Experimental. 17 built. Late 1941
SC, SC-1	AS	7.5ft × 8.5ft mattress	Primarily DDs, CLs & CAs. Early 1942
SC-3	AS	15ft × 4.5ft mattress	Improved SC-1. 1942
SG	SS	48ft × 15° parabola	Small, low-mounted antenna. April 1942
Mk 3 (FC)	FC	12ft × 3ft cyl. section	Main battery. Oct. 1941
Mk 4 (FD)	FC	6ft × 6ft dual parabola	DP, with Mk 37 director. Sept 1941
Mk 8 (FH)	FC	10ft × 3.6ft polyrod	Replaced FC

Notes: AS=Air Search; SS=Surface Search; FC=Fire Control. The designations used for US Navy radars need some explanation. Search radars and fire control radars were under the control of different naval bureaux, BuShips and BuOrd respectively. BuShips used, for the most part, a two-letter system of designators. The first letter indicated function (e.g. 'S' for search) and the second the position in the development sequence ('A' for the first of a type, etc.). Thus the third production search radar was the SC. BuOrd used a simple mark system for the fire control radars. However, early fire control radars often carried designations in both systems. Thus the Mk 8 fire control radar was also called the FH.

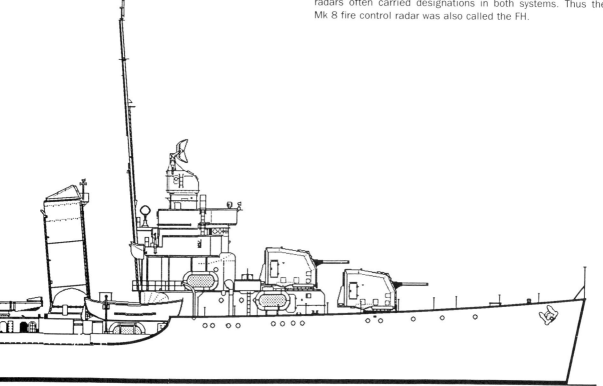

PRINCIPAL COMBATANT CLASSES, 1942–3

Country	Class	Type	Displacement (tons)	Length oa (ft)	Beam (ft)	Belt (in)	Max. speed (kt)	Cruising speed (kt)	Range (nm)	Armament	Year of launch
USA	*North Carolina*	BB	37,484	728.6	108.3	12	28	15	17,450	9×16in, 20×5in	1940
Japan	*Kongo*	BB*	32,000	738.5	95.2	8	30.5	18	10,000	8×14in, 14×6in, 8×5in	1912
USA	*Yorktown*	CV	19,875	824.6	83.2	5	32.5	15	12,000	8×5in, 96 aircraft	1936
Japan	*Shokaku*	CV	25,675	844.8	85.3	6.5	34.2	18	9,700	16×5in, 72 aircraft	1939
USA	*New Orleans*	CA	10,136	588	61.6	5	32.7	15	10,000	9×8in, 8×5in	1933
Japan	*Furutaka*	CA	7,100	607.5	51.7	3	34.5	14	8,000	6×8in	1925
Japan	*Nachi*	CA	10,000	668.5	56.9	3.9	35.5	14	8,000	10×8in, 6×4.7in	1927
USA	*Atlanta*	CL	6,718	541.5	53.2	3.7	32.5	15	8,500	16×5in	1941
USA	*Brooklyn*	CL	9,767	608.3	61.6	5	32.5	15	10,000	15×6in, 8×5in	1936
Japan	*Sendai*	CL	5,195	534.6	48.4	2.5	35.2	10	7,800	7×5.5in	1925
USA	*Benson*	DD	1,839	348.3	36.1	–	35	12	6,500	4×5in, 5×21in TT	1939
Japan	*Asashio*	DD	1,961	388	33.9	–	35	10	5,700	6×5in, 8×24in TT	1936

*The *Kongo* class fast battleships were built as battlecruisers to a British design; they were improved *Tigers*.

NEW ORLEANS

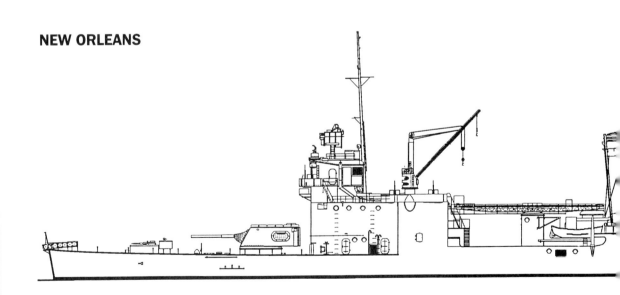

THE MAJOR COMBAT AREA
IN THE SOUTH PACIFIC

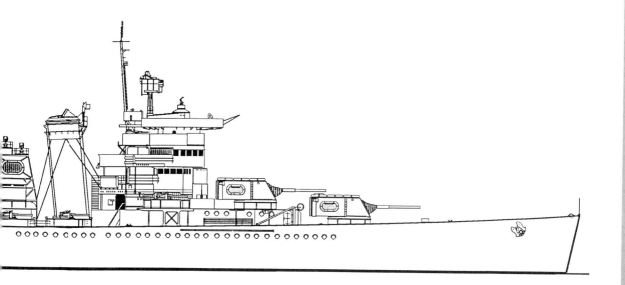

1.	Battle of Savo Island	9 August 1942
2.	Battle of Eastern Solomons	22–4 August 1942
3.	Battle of Cape Esperance	11–12 October 1942
4.	Battle of Santa Cruz	25–6 October 1942
5.	Battle of Gaudalcanal – I	13 November 1942
6.	Battle of Guadalcanal – II	14–15 November 1942
7.	Battle of Tassafaronga	30 November to 1 December 1942
8.	Battle of Kula Gulf	6 July 1943
9.	Battle of Kolombangara	13 July 1943
10.	Battle of Vella Gulf	6 August 1943
11.	Battle of Vella Lavella	6–7 October 1943
12.	Battle of Empress Augusta Bay	2 November 1943

▲53

53. There were eleven submarines based at Casablanca at the time of the 'Torch' invasions. Three fell victim to air attack in the first minutes of the invasion, while four of the remaining eight actually carried out attacks on the invasion fleet in support of the sorting destroyers although none of the torpedoes hit home. Four of the submarines were lost during these attacks and the subsequent action before the fighting ended on the 15th; one of them is seen here on the rocks near Casablanca. (USN/NARS)

▼54

54. The forces deployed during the 'Torch' invasions gathered at Casablanca after the fighting stopped. The destroyer *Cole* (DD155) is seen here pulling into port after her action at Safi. In the background, to the right, are the escort carrier *Chenango* (CVE28), with the cruiser *Augusta* (CA31) behind her. *Augusta* could be readily identified because she wore the rare Ms.17 dazzle-pattern camouflage. (USN/NARS)

55. The other side of *Augusta*, with *Chenango* behind her and the transport *Leonard Wood* (AP25) to the left, in Casablanca harbour, November 1942. This is a good view of the rare Ms.17 camouflage scheme. The splinter pattern of four tones of purple-blue shows a marked British influence. (USN/NARS)

56. Some unfinished business was being wrapped up at Pearl Harbor during this period with the raising of the battleships sunk on 7 December 1941. The first to be raised was *Nevada* (BB36) – seen here being pumped out on 17 February 1942 – because she had been beached at the edge of the main channel into the harbour. The next day she was moved into dry dock, where her numerous holes were patched over the next month. (Via Bob Cressman)

57. The most heavily damaged battleship to be rebuilt was *West Virginia* (BB49). She had been hit by as many as seven torpedoes in rapid succession and had sunk so fast that she hadn't had a chance to capsize. Nevertheless she was raised during May 1942 and was dry-docked on 9 June. As with the other raised battleships, temporary repairs were performed, sufficient for the ship to make the West Coast under her own power. There permanent repairs and some needed modernization were performed. Three other old battleships sunk at Pearl Harbor were not rebuilt, either because of the extent of the damage or because of their age. (USN/NARS)

55▲

56▲   57▼

▲58

▲59   ▼60

58. Action continued unabated in the Solomons after the Battle of Santa Cruz. Reinforcement runs continued daily, the Americans making theirs during the day and the Japanese coming in at night. On 12 November the Japanese sent in a major force led by the two fast battleships *Hiei* and *Kirishima* along with a light cruiser and fourteen destroyers, with the intention of shelling Henderson Field that night. The Americans had run in a supply convoy that day and the covering forces, consisting of two heavy cruisers, three light cruisers and eight destroyers, stayed in the area. The American forces were disposed in line ahead with the cruisers betweeen two groups of four destroyers. *Aaron Ward* (DD483), shown, led the aft group. Both sides took a beating in the 34-minute mêlée that followed, the Americans in particular: only two ships in the American force, one destroyer and one light cruiser, got through the battle without major damage. *Aaron Ward* was not a member of that lucky pair. She was quickly thrown on her own by the disintegration of the American formation and, heading towards the battle, she came under fire from unknown Japanese warships at about 0230. Within a few minutes she was hit by nine shells, one of which struck her below the waterline, flooding her engine room. She was dead in the water and out of the fight. At dawn she was taken in tow in the direction of Tulagi. (USN/NARS)

59. The heavy cruiser *Portland* (CA33) was another casualty in the dark on 13 November 1942. She survived the opening blows of the battle that knocked out three of the American cruisers and was in the middle of a gunfight with *Hiei* when she was hit by a torpedo that took off a screw and left her unable to steer. *Hiei*'s encounters with the American cruisers resulted in multiple holes in her own thinly armoured skin, damaging her steering gear and leaving her, also, unable to manoeuvre. The fates of the two disabled warships were completely different, thanks to American control of the air: *Portland* managed to make sufficient repairs to limp into Tulagi harbour, but *Hiei* was swarmed over by Marine Dauntlesses and damaged to such an extent that she had to be scuttled at 1800.

60. The flagship of Rear Admiral Callaghan at the Naval Battle of Guadalcanal was the heavy cruiser *San Francisco* (CA38). Towards the end of the mêlée *San Francisco* found herself in a duel with unfortunate *Hiei*. *Kirishima*, momentarily disengaged, found *Hiei*'s tormentor with her big 14in guns, sending as many as twelve heavy shells into the cruiser's superstructure. One of these shells killed Callaghan and *San Franciso*'s captain. (USN/NARS)

61. Despite the damage to her superstructure, *San Francisco* remained basically sound and steamed from the scene under her own power along with the undamaged light cruiser *Helena* (CL50), the wounded *Juneau* (CL52) and the three operational destroyers. Just south of Guadalcanal they ran into *I26*, which put a torpedo into *Juneau*. The already damaged cruiser literally disintegrated. That loss put the toll for the day for the Americans at two cruisers and four destroyers sunk; the Japanese lost *Hiei* and two destroyers. In this photograph *San Francisco* is seen entering Pearl Harbor on 4 December 1942, her war over for a while. (USN/NARS)

61▲

62. A close-up photograph of the bridge of *San Francisco*, taken at the same time as the preceding photograph. The damage has been patched up on the surface but was sufficient to keep the cruiser out of action until May 1943, when she reappeared in the Aleutians. She missed the reprise of the Naval Battle of Guadalcanal. Two nights after the first battle, the Japanese sent *Kirishima* down the Slot again. This time the Americans had two battleships, *South Dakota* (BB57) and *Washington* (BB56), in the way. When the smoke cleared, *Kirishima* had been sunk and *South Dakota* damaged. (USN/NARS)

62 ▼

63. After the twin Battles of Guadalcanal, the Japanese concluded that they would not be able to continue the practice of running in supplies with conventional transport vessels. Thus, in order to supply their troops on the island, they adopted a novel approach, loading large drums with supplies which were to be pushed overboard from destroyers speeding along the shore and float ashore with the tide. The first run of eight supply destroyers came on the night of 30 November 1942. The Americans opposed the enemy with TF67, composed of four heavy cruisers, including *New Orleans* (CA32), shown, a light cruiser and six destroyers. (USN/NARS)

▲63   ▼64

64. This time the Americans had every advantage: the preponderance of firepower was on their side; six of the Japanese destroyers were encumbered with supply drums; and the US ships had radar and used it to advantage, pinpointing the oncoming Japanese long before they themselves were seen. The lead American destroyers unleashed a full salvo of torpedoes and the cruisers opened fire before the Japanese were even aware of their presence. Nevertheless, the Japanese reacted with practised coolness. The Americans concentrated their fire on the lead Japanese destroyer, *Takanami*. The rest split into small groups, some dropping their supply canisters as planned and turning for home, others launching torpedo salvoes at the Americans before they, too, turned away. The torpedoes wreaked havoc. *New Orleans* took a single hit in the bow that ignited her forward magazines and sheared off her bow between the forward turrets. (USN/NARS)

65. The three remaining heavy cruisers also took hits that caused serious damage. One of them, *Northampton* (CA26) sank at 0300. *New Orleans* had to beach at Tulagi to prevent her sinking: she is seen here sometime in December, covered with camouflage netting to protect her from observation. (USMC)

66. Tired of slugging it out with the stubborn Japanese along the Tassafaronga, the Americans decided to start the New Year with an end run, a landing on the west coast of Guadalcanal that would bring up troops behind the defenders. The convoy bringing in the troops was escorted by a veteran group of cruisers, including *Chicago* (CA29), shown here with *Louisville* (CA28) behind her in a photograph taken from *Wichita* (CA45) on 29 January 1943. Soon after this photograph was taken, near Rennel Island, the convoy was jumped by Japanese aircraft which put a pair of torpedoes into *Chicago*. The other two cruisers were also hit, in both cases the torpedoes, mercifully, failed to explode. (USN/NARS)

67. *Chicago* was under tow back towards Espiritu Santo on the 20th when she was found by another wave of Japanese attackers. This time they put four more torpedoes into the old cruiser, already low in the water, and sent her to the bottom. The landings on the west coast of Guadalcanal took place on schedule on 1 February 1943. They proved to be unnecessary. The Japanese had decided on the last day of 1942 to abandon the island and began a beautifully executed evacuation of their troops on the same day as the west coast landings. On three nights between 1 and 7 February they ran in as many as twenty destroyers, pulling out almost 11,000 troops without the Americans having a clue. (USN/NARS)

65▲

66▲   67▼

▲68

68. As the tide of Japanese advances was being stopped in the Solomons, American naval forces were gathering in the North Pacific to push back the enemy in the Aleutians. This campaign had a much different flavour from that in the South Pacific. Here the weather was as much the enemy as the warships of the opposing side. Here, also, air power played a much reduced role. During the first months of 1943, the US Navy put together a fleet of primarily older warships, many of them veterans of the Solomons, to contest the waters in the Aleutians. The first action came on 26 March 1943 when a small force of American vessels led by the heavy cruiser *Salt Lake City* (CA25), shown here, intercepted a Japanese convoy headed for Attu. The convoy turned back, but its escort force engaged the Americans. In probably the only pure gunfire daylight engagement of the Pacific war, the two sides pounded each other at long range for over three hours. *Salt Lake City* was heavily damaged, at one point in the battle drifting without power, as was the Japanese cruiser *Nachi*. Ultimately both sides turned for home as magazines emptied and fear of enemy aircraft increased. No ships were lost, but the failure of the Japanese to resupply Attu marked the beginning of the end of their tenuous foothold in the Aleutians. (USN/NHC)

69. In April 1943 forces began to gather at Kuluk Bay, Adak, for Operation 'Landcrab', the invasion of Attu. The heavy cruiser *Louisville* (CA28) was one of a number of Solomons veterans sent into the inhospitable waters of the Aleutians; she is seen here at Kuluk Bay on 25 April 1943. (USN/NARS)

▼69

70. Another veteran heavy cruiser *Wichita* (CA45), is also seen at Kuluk Bay; the low-lying clouds are a near-permanent feature of weather in the Aleutians. The invasion of Attu, actually closer to Japan than the other Japanese garrison at Kiska, took place on 11 May 1943. This 'leapfrogging' of enemy garrisons in order to isolate major strongpoints became standard practice in the Central Pacific campaign. The conquest of the small enemy force on Attu took longer than expected, not being complete until 28 May. (USN/NARS)

71. The finale in the Aleutians was an anti-climax. After the bitter struggle for Attu, the Allies expected another fierce fight to shift the Japanese from their last toehold at Kiska. A large naval force was assembled, composed, as before, largely of older warships, such as the rebuilt Pearl Harbor victim *Tennessee* (BB43), seen here at Adak, along with a variety of other members of the landing force, three days before the invasion on 12 August 1943. It turned out that the Japanese had abandoned the island, unknown to the Allies, nineteen days before the invasion. A total of 35,000 troops stormed ashore, greeted only by a handful of stray dogs.

72. The successful invasion of North Africa in November 1942 and the subsequent capture of Tunisia led to planning for the next Allied moves in Europe. Against some serious Americans reservations, the British pushed through a Mediterranean strategy that called for the invasion of Sicily as the next step. Naval vessels, such as *Arkansas* (BB33), gathered at North African ports during June 1943, forming the invasion fleet. Waiting in Oran, *Arkansas*'s crew filled every available perch to get a glimpse of a USO show. Note the variety of radars visible on *Arkansas* and the unidentified vessel docked behind her. The battleship has a Mk 3 (FC) antenna on her foretop and an SG on her short mainmast. The hidden vessel has an SC antenna on the nearer of the two visible masts and an SG and an SC-2 on the other. (USN/NARS)

▲73

73. Although the invasion fleet had only to cross the Mediterranean in order to land its forces, the supplies and troops still had to cross the Atlantic to reach their staging areas. Given the great success of the German U-boat operations during 1941 and 1942, the passage of the

▼74

Atlantic was risky at best. However, the opening months of 1943 saw a dramatic reversal in the U-boat war, due in great measure to the arrival of small escort aircraft carriers (CVEs). *Bogue* (CVE9), seen in here in April 1943, was the second US Navy CVE and the first assigned

to ASW duties. (USN/NARS)

74. The veteran ex-destroyer *Greene* (AVD-13, ex-DD26) was part of *Bogue*'s original task group. In its first operation, *Bogue*'s group was positioned in the middle of convoy HX228 from 5 to 14 March 1943, where

they proved largely ineffective. It was soon learned that CVE groups operated most effectively at the edges of convoys, free to chase down U-boat contacts. *Greene* carries an SC radar antenna at the top of her foremast, with an SE lower on the mast. (USN/NARS)

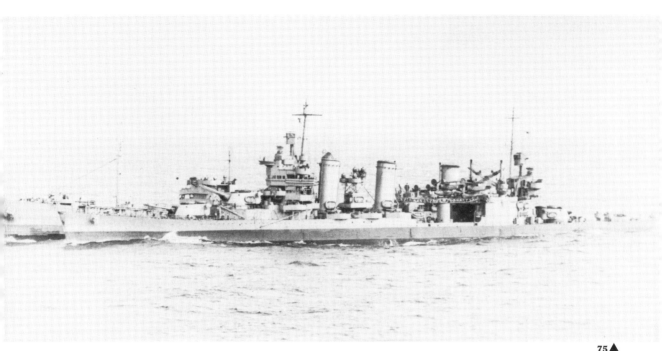

75 ▲

75. While the invasion of North Africa took the Axis by surprise, there was no way that the Allies could hope to conceal the preparations for the next invasion: the build-up of shipping in the Mediterranean was too big to hide. Nevertheless, a small diversion was considered appropriate. On 18 July 1943, two days before the planned invasion of Sicily, a combined force of US and Royal Navy warships closed the coast of Norway, hoping to distract the Germans. One of the participants was the heavy cruiser *Tuscaloosa* (CA37), seen here refuelling from *Chicopee* (AO34). (USN/NARS)

76. Another participant in the diversion off Norway was the brand new battleship *Alabama* (BB60). She finished working up in June and moved to Scapa Flow, where she was joined by the patched-up *South Dakota* (BB57) in time for the diversion. By January 1944 *Alabama* had been transferred to the Pacific, where she spent the rest of the war. (USN/NARS)

76 ▼

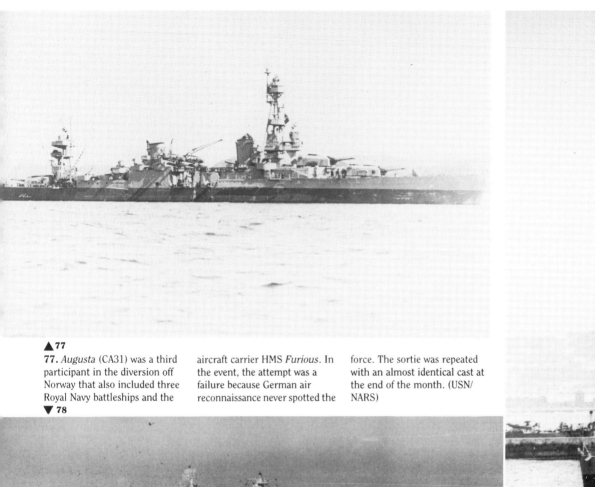

▲ 77

77. *Augusta* (CA31) was a third participant in the diversion off Norway that also included three Royal Navy battleships and the aircraft carrier HMS *Furious*. In the event, the attempt was a failure because German air reconnaissance never spotted the force. The sortie was repeated with an almost identical cast at the end of the month. (USN/ NARS)

▼ 78

78. The Sicily invasion was one of the few occasions when warships were able to influence a land engagement. So much of the battle zone in Sicily lay within range of ship's artillery that support vessels like the light cruiser *Birmingham* (CL62) were called on repeatedly to intervene in land battles. (USN/NARS)

79. An even better example of this phenomenon is represented by the light cruiser *Savannah* (CL42) which, along with *Boise* (CL47, rebuilt after the beating she took at the Battle of Cape Esperance in October 1942), halted a counterattack by German armour near Gela on 12 July 1943. *Savannah* is seen here

the next day at Algiers, where she had retired to replenish. A supply ship which had caught fire in the port burns in the background. (USN/NARS)

▲80

80. The last major naval operation in the Mediterranean was the invasion of the Italian mainland at Salerno on 9 September 1943. As was the case during the Sicily invasions, naval forces were able to intervene directly in land battles. In this case the intervention was crucial, turning the tide for the Allies. The destroyer *Mayo* (DD422), in this photograph refuelling from the light aircraft carrier *Independence* (CVL22), was part of force that intervened decisively on 13 September. (USN/NARS)

▼81

81. The move to break out of the beach-head at Salerno was so slow to develop that the Germans had adequate time to react. A force of three German armoured divisions assaulted the landing force and threatened to push the Allied troops back into the water. *Mayo* and other US and Royal Navy forces shelled the advancing armour, halting the German forces and giving the defenders enough time to regroup. (USN/NARS)

82. The complete conquest of Guadalcanal set the stage for the immediate movement of Allied forces up the Solomon chain. The next Japanese strongholds to the north were on the islands of New Georgia and Kolombangara on either side of Kula Gulf. The US began sending forces into Kula Gulf in March 1943. On 6 March, three light cruisers, including Cleveland (CL55) and three destroyers steamed into Kula Gulf to shell the Japanese airfield at Vila on Kolombangara.

83. On 30 June 1943 troops of the US 43rd Infantry Division were landed on Rendova Island. *Pringle (DD477)* was part of the force that shelled the Shortland Islands on the 29th and then supported the Rendova landings on the 30th. She was one of a limited number of *Fletcher* Class destroyers that were configured to handle OS2U aircraft. They sacrificed No. 3 turret, putting a steam catapult in its place. (USN/NHC)

84. The battleship *North Carolina* (BB55) also formed part of the cover for the landings on Rendova. She had been out of action since September 1942 when she was torpedoed. The landings on Rendova were a prelude to an assault on Munda, the main Japanese base on New Georgia. On 4 July 1943 troops were transported across the channel to Bairoko on New Georgia. (USAF)

82▲

83▲   84▼

▲85

▲86 ▼87

85. The night following the landings on New Georgia, the US Navy deployed three light cruisers and four destroyers into Kula Gulf to oppose the expected Japanese reaction. Predictably, the Japanese sent a force of ten destroyers, seven of which were loaded with troops for Munda. This photograph, taken from *Honolulu* (CL48), shows *Helena* (CL50), next behind in line, at the moment of her destruction. *Helena* was hit by three torpedoes simultaneously, breaking her in two. Despite this loss, the attack on Munda continued, the airstrip falling to the Americans on 5 August. (USN/NARS)

86. After a year of lessons from the Japanese in night fighting, the Americans finally reached the point where they could take on the enemy's destroyer forces on even terms. Six US destroyers, including *Maury* (DD401), under Cdr Moosbrugger intercepted four Japanese destroyers carrying troops for Vila on the night of 6 August 1943. Using radar and improved tactics, the Americans sank three of the Japanese while suffering no damage. (USN/NARS)

87. The northernmost major island in the Solomons chain is Bougainville. On 1 November 1943 landings took place at Cape Torokina aimed at capturing the airfields there as a launching point for raids on Rabaul. That night a Japanese force of one heavy cruiser, two light cruisers and six destroyers raided Empress Augusta Bay, attempting to disrupt the landings. The American force of four light cruisers, including the new *Columbia* (CL56), and eight destroyers intercepted the intruders. By the end of the mêlée two Japanese vessels had been sunk and two US cruisers damaged. The landing force was never in danger. (USN/NARS)

88. At the same time as the Torokina landings, US carrier forces staged raids on Buna and Buka on New Guinea. TF38 was formed around *Saratoga* (CV3), seen here en route to Rabaul, the next stop for the task force. Rabaul was raided by carrier aircraft from *Saratoga* and *Princeton* (CVL23) on 4 November 1943, damage being inflicted on four heavy cruisers and one light cruiser. (USN/NARS)

89. The campaign in the Solomons ended with the landings on Cape Gloucester at the western tip of New Britain on the day after Christmas 1943. Rabaul is located at the opposite end of this island. The troops were transported to the landing beaches in LCIs. (USMC)

90. The capture of Cape Gloucester breached the barrier of the Bismarck Archipelago and isolated Rabaul. It effectively marked the end of the drive that had started with the landings on Guadalcanal sixteen months earlier. There would be further landings on New Guinea and elsewhere in the South Pacific, but the focus of US naval operations now shifted to the Central Pacific and the line of island bastions that led directly to Japan. (USMC)

88▲

89▲   90▼

The *Fotofax* series

A new range of pictorial studies of military subjects for the modeller, historian and enthusiast. Each title features a carefully-selected set of photographs plus a data section of facts and figures on the topic covered. With line drawings and detailed captioning, every volume represents a succinct and valuable study of the subject. New and forthcoming titles:

Warbirds
F-111 Aardvark
P-47 Thunderbolt
B-52 Stratofortress
Stuka!
Jaguar
US Strategic Air Power:
  Europe 1942–1945
Dornier Bombers
RAF in Germany

Vintage Aircraft
German Naval Air Service
Sopwith Camel
Fleet Air Arm, 1920–1939
German Bombers of WWI

Soldiers
World War One: 1914
World War One: 1915
World War One: 1916
Union Forces of the American
  Civil War
Confederate Forces of the
  American Civil War
Luftwaffe Uniforms
British Battledress 1945–1967
  (2 vols)

Warships
Japanese Battleships, 1897–
  1945
Escort Carriers of World War
  Two
German Battleships, 1897–
  1945
Soviet Navy at War, 1941–1945
US Navy in World War Two,
  1943–1944
US Navy, 1946–1980 (2 vols)
British Submarines of World
  War One

Military Vehicles
The Chieftain Tank
Soviet Mechanized Firepower
  Today
British Armoured Cars since
  1945
NATO Armoured Fighting
  Vehicles
The Road to Berlin
NATO Support Vehicles

The *Illustrated* series

The internationally successful range of photo albums devoted to current, recent and historic topics, compiled by leading authors and representing the best means of obtaining your own photo archive.

Warbirds
US Spyplanes
USAF Today
Strategic Bombers, 1945–1985
Air War over Germany
Mirage
US Naval and Marine Aircraft
  Today
USAAF in World War Two
B-17 Flying Fortress
Tornado
Junkers Bombers of World War
  Two
Argentine Air Forces in the
  Falklands Conflict
F-4 Phantom Vol II
Army Gunships in Vietnam
Soviet Air Power Today
F-105 Thunderchief
Fifty Classic Warbirds
Canberra and B-57
German Jets of World War Two

Vintage Warbirds
The Royal Flying Corps in
  World War One
German Army Air Service in
  World War One
RAF between the Wars
The Bristol Fighter
Fokker Fighters of World War
  One
Air War over Britain, 1914–
  1918
Nieuport Aircraft of World War
  One

Tanks
Israeli Tanks and Combat
  Vehicles
Operation Barbarossa
Afrika Korps
Self-Propelled Howitzers
British Army Combat Vehicles
  1945 to the Present
The Churchill Tank
US Mechanized Firepower
  Today
Hitler's Panzers
Panzer Armee Afrika
US Marine Tanks in World War
  Two

Warships
The Royal Navy in 1980s
The US Navy Today
NATO Navies of the 1980s
British Destroyers in World
  War Two
Nuclear Powered Submarines
Soviet Navy Today
British Destroyers in World
  War One
The World's Aircraft Carriers,
  1914–1945
The Russian Convoys, 1941–
  1945
The US Navy in World War
  Two
British Submarines in World
  War Two
British Cruisers in World War
  One
U-Boats of World War Two
Malta Convoys, 1940–1943

Uniforms
US Special Forces of World
  War Two
US Special Forces 1945 to the
  Present
The British Army in Northern
  Ireland
Israeli Defence Forces, 1948 to
  the Present
British Special Forces, 1945 to
  Present
US Army Uniforms Europe,
  1944–1945
The French Foreign Legion
Modern American Soldier
Israeli Elite Units
US Airborne Forces of World
  War Two
The Boer War
The Commandos World War
  Two to the Present
Victorian Colonial Wars

A catalogue listing these series and other Arms & Armour Press titles is available on request from: Sales Department, Arms & Armour Press, Artillery House, Artillery Row, London SW1P 1RT.